$\mathcal{L}$imericks
New & Naughty!

To Peter —

This isn't exactly "Hiawatha,"
But then, I'm not exactly Longfellow!

Enjoy — and don't blush too much.
Hopefully it'll bring back happy memories
of Prospect Street.

All good wishes,

Chick

AKA Al Kracht

Limericks

New & Naughty!

Over 240
original limericks
by Al Kracht

With illustrations
by Paula Brinkman Hughes

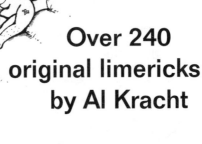

Limerick
Lane
Press, Inc.

Published by Limerick Lane Press, Inc.
5 Birch Lane, Chappaqua, New York 10514, USA.

Cover and type design by Ryder & Schild, Inc., Miami, Florida

Printed by Goulet Printery, Inc., Winsted, Connecticut

Library of Congress Catalog Card Number 97-94117

Kracht, Al
   Limericks New & Naughty! — Over 240 Original Limericks by Al Kracht
      Poetry
      Humor

ISBN 0-9659808-0-4

   First Edition — December 1997

   Printed in the United States of America

   10 9 8 7 6 5 4 3 2 1

I **inscribe** this fun book to my wife,
Forty-six years we're married, sans strife;
And to those other lasses,
With whom I've worked, joked, made passes,
Whose fond urgings helped bring it to life.

The **limerick,** down through the Ages,
Has charmed writers, and leaders, and sages,
And "the man in the street" —
All choose some to repeat —
We trust you'll find more on these pages.

Introduction

The first time I can recall hearing a limerick was at a dinner party at my parents' home, when dear Aunt Paula — an "Auntie Mame" type who lived with us — reeled off "There was a young man from Boston..." during the dessert-time banter. I was nearly eleven at the time, had discovered light verse in *The Saturday Evening Post,* and in *Popular Science,* of all places, but this limerick — and some others tossed back at her by those present — opened a new door for me.

I was intrigued — I now guess — with the multiple rhymes, the subject matter, the mental images they evoked, the surprise ending, and their ease of memorability. To this day I know limerick lovers can simply ask "Have you heard the one about 'The lad from St. Paul?' and they'll quickly get a "yes" or "no" response, or their friend will say, "I know of one. What's yours?"

Also, since my parents were born in Europe and knew several languages (with a habit of substituting German or Spanish counterparts for any American word that didn't immediately come to mind), it became natural for me to want to add to my English vocabulary. Words found in poems became a prime focus in this endeavor — perhaps because they stood out so much more visually than words lodged in a page of prose text, or that so much more significance, and perhaps hilarity, was to be found in them. And, of course, the many sexual connotations.

I enjoyed finding limericks, reading limericks, and writing limericks, and that pleasure has lasted all my life. In junior high — thanks probably to an imaginative teacher/advisor — our yearbook was printed in verse, each classmate selecting another to write about, and that's where a limerick of mine first saw publication. In high school I submitted them to the school paper, entertained my friends with them — and they put up with me.

At Princeton, I belonged to Key and Seal Club, an eating club that had a tradition of members singing ribald college songs in its cozy paneled bar room, all the more alive on party weekends when the ladies were on hand. This was in the immediate post World War II era, when many fellow classmates were returning war vets, who added colorful songs and verses they had picked up in the service.

We'd go through a whole evening of singing — ranging from "Roll Your Leg Over," to "Lydia Pinkham," to "Little Mary Murphy," to "Her Mother Never Told Her," to "Alouette," to "The Deacon Went Down," plus many others — and, eventually, someone would start on the chorus for endless rounds of limericks, which ran —

> "Iy, yi, yi-yi! —
> In China they never serve chili,
>> Now, here comes another verse
>> That's worse than the other verse,
> So, waltz me around again, Willie!"

By now, many of those verses we sang 50 years ago have become fairly well known. Scratching my memory, I'd say that the dozen most frequently sung back then were:

1) The young lady from Norway
2) The couple named Kelly
3) A painter named Titian McSpadder
4) The lesbian out of Khartoum
5) The young nun from Peru
6) The old monk from Siberia
7) The young maid from Alsace
8) The young man named McNair
9) The old whore from Detroit
10) The young lady named Alice
11) The old whore named Hester
12) The young man from Kent

My suspicion is that, if you're reading this Introduction, you probably know these yourself. If not, I've included them in their entirety in the Appendix. My aim here is to supply a new and completely original assortment.

At the Key and Seal parties, it was tradition for anyone singing a limerick verse to look 'round the room filled with perhaps 50 guys and their dates, and point to a fellow member to come up with the next verse. If he (or his date) could not immediately provide an as yet unsung stanza, they had to pay for the next round of beers, drinks, etc. Naturally, it didn't take long for all 90 Key and Seal members to learn a few popular limericks, and be on the hunt for a new and sensational one to toss into the fray the next time around. There's a larder full of such in this book — limericks I've written in the years since graduation. Too bad Key and Seal Club is no longer in existence; its members would have found a mother lode here.

As I moved into the business arena in New York City, as a newspaper representative calling on advertising agencies, I discovered one worldly media buyer — at the then prestigious Benton & Bowles agency — who would rarely grant representatives an audience if they didn't have a new off-color limerick for her. Then, when I became an ad agency executive, there were clients who were intrigued with salty limericks. *Business Week* magazine ran an advertising industry contest, based on limerick submissions, to promote its virtues, and compiled a book of the entries.

Down through the years, friends and acquaintances would request bawdy limericks of me, for their use in unique situations. The late Joe O'Connor, a dear friend who sold hydraulic systems to NASA, had to deal with a purchasing agent who set up the same requirements as that lady media buyer at Benton & Bowles had years before — and turned to me to help him out.

Now, in my primary business of writing customized light verse for folks in the U.S. and other English-speaking countries — generally to be read aloud at birthdays, anniversaries, retirement parties, weddings, award ceremonies, and the like — I'm in daily contact with a host of limerick lovers. While the light verse they require necessitates a less constrained rhyme scheme, and calls for substantially longer verse, many people make it a point to ask for, and swap their own, limerick verses, as part of the interplay between us.

For example, Harry Franke, the ebullient senior partner in the sizeable old Milwaukee law firm of Cook & Franke, invariably includes one or more limericks with his correspondence, not just to me, but to a wide group of friends with whom he exchanges missives of merriment. And, Dale Messick, the now 91-year-old cartoonist who for years provided us with the peppy "Brenda Starr" comic strip, called out of the blue to congratulate me on an article in *The Wall Street Journal,* and offered this limerick of her own, using her christened name, Dalia:

> A lovely young lady named Dalia,
> Was wooed by a guy from Australia;
> > He took her to Perth,
> > But he wasn't worth
> Any look at her paraphernalia!

Dale, who now calls herself "Granny Glamour," and does cartoons in that vein, has this advice for us all aiming for advanced age: "If you quit, and just sit — that's it!"

Yes, there's a legion of limerick lovers out there, many of whom have created topical and fun verses, the way Harry and Dale have. This book represents my "going public" with many I have penned over the years — and I'd welcome hearing from all of you who are willing to share your efforts with a receptive ear.

I hope you enjoy my creations.

> Al Kracht
> Chappaqua, NY — 1997

My **suggestion,** to read this book right,
Is to stick with eight verses a night,
And, that way you'll reap
A month's happy sleep —
It's not meant to be read in one flight.

The mores of life come and go,
As history always will show,
    And, what's "right" today
    Will forever betray
How much — and how little — we know.

A **tipsy** young maiden from Corning,
Found six guys in her bed in the morning;
Said she, "I don't mind,
For they've all been so kind,
And each didn't come without warning!"

19

*I*n court, the young call girl, Miss Schrader,
Maintained that Sir Arthur had laid her;
    And, Sir Arthur was good,
    She would want understood,
But not so the check he had paid her.

A suave politician was Norton,
And fair to the girls he was courtin';
    He'd take three to bed,
    Let each give him head —
They deserve equal time if you're sportin'.

*M*y young reindeer," explained poor old Santa,
"Has developed a rather weird canter;
    It's nothing I've taught,
    Just his mother was caught
By a stallion down in Atlanta."

*I*n the crowds, the golf pro would spot her,
One day in the tall rough he got her,
  As he zipped up to leave,
  She said with some peeve,
"I thought this hole you'd play a two-shotter!"

*T*he old duffer, so eager to sin,
Couldn't raise his staff, to his chagrin;
And the call girl he paid,
As he sought to get laid,
Laughed, and said, "Never up, never in!"

*T*he sexy come-ons of Miss Frith,
In bed proved entirely a myth;
She'd simply lie there,
As if she didn't care,
Which made her no fun to be with.

*O*ne trouble with modern militia,
Is they hate sex, and won't let me kiss ya;
So, I want you to know,
If you're aching to go,
And do join their ranks, babe, I'll miss ya!

*T*he **breasts** of the buxom Miss Stokes,
Float buoyantly each time she soaks;
    That's as it should be,
    Except she has three,
Which makes her the butt of crude jokes!

I **just have** to tell you, Saint Peter
Is no longer our Heaven's greeter;
    He could not get a raise —
    Which God's frozen these days —
So he went for a deal that was sweeter.

*O***ver-heated** forever was Barb,
So she'd wear just the lightest of garb;
    Which the guys thought okay,
    'Cause her looks made their day,
If she caught cold, there's always bi-carb!

A **stalwart** young stud name of Lew,
Was considered an excellent screw;
    And not just, girls say,
    For his strength as a lay,
But for all other things he would do.

I **dedicate** this little verse,
To each special doctor and nurse,
Who can manage to smile
Through a day that is vile,
And care more for my health than my purse!

*S*aid the recovering spinster, Miss Lear,
To the surgeon she'd come to revere,
"When you put in that heart,
You gave me a fresh start,
But I've now got this craving for beer!"

*S*aid a luscious cock-sucker, named Skip,
"Let me give all you doctors a tip;
I've tried pills, drops, and spray,
But find this the best way
To cut through my post-nasal drip."

*F*or rampant sex prowess, I'm told,
Subway Sam was the one to behold;
He'd find a pretty strap-hanger,
Slide behind her, and bang her,
But so well that she never would scold.

 Her **short skirt** revealed a rare view,
 He stared, as commuters will do;
 "You're no gentleman," gasped she,
 He replied, "Believe me,
 I can see that you aren't one, too!"

Some girls in short skirts made of leather,
Are disposed to make you wonder "whether;"
But you'd better not say
That they all feel that way,
And, they're changeable, too, like the weather.

"**C**ome inside me," she said with a squeal,
"I'm dying to know how you feel.
I've dreamed lots about it —
I'm sure you don't doubt it —
Now I do want to have it for real."

(time passes)

"**I**'m coming," she whispered, "Oh my!,"
"Together," he answered, "Let's try,"
So they stepped up the pace,
'Til their loving embrace
Blazed with starbursts all over the sky!

The **guests** of the Sultan of Turkey
All swam in a pool that was murky,
So you couldn't quite see
Who had goosed you or me,
And it turned out the Sultan was quirky.

*A*n **acrobat** brimming with zest,
Puts girls that he dates to the test;
He props each up in bed,
Points his cock where she's spread,
And somersaults into her nest!

A **horny** old maid from St. Kitts,
Always keeps her legs crossed as she knits;
    Her crotch holds her wool,
    And with each little pull,
She gives her cunt secretive twits.

The **aging** call girl, named McRae,
Tried things so her business would stay;
    She had breast reduction,
    Face lifts, liposuction —
Good God if it ever gives way!

They **took** multi-birth pills, hoped quadruplets,
Were amazed when the Doc said "septuplets;"
    But luckily found,
    'Twasn't them, but their hound,
Lady Bess, who was having her puplets!

*T*he slow pace of his wife's pet "Soaps,"
Has affected their sex play, Sam mopes;
So, if they screw tonight,
And she shows real delight,
She'll climax next Tuesday — he hopes!

A scrumptious young model named Peggy,
Is lovely, and lissome, and leggy,
She leads a great life,
Which with menfolk is rife,
But makes sure that she doesn't get "preggy."

*M*oonshiners in Kentucky's back hills,
Are exceedingly proud of their stills;
But no way can you
Ever sample their brew,
Shootin' strangers is one of their skills.

An amorous young lady named Florence,
Has a climax that comes in great torrents,
   And washes her mate
   Out past the front gate,
Which is more than such lovemaking warrants!

The orgies in some college dorms,
Have prompted most stringent reforms,
Now, coeds who lay
More than three guys a day,
Are expelled for exceeding the norms.

A **healthy** young scholar name Boris,
Read so much of Homer and Horace,
That, to honor each screw —
Which he found time to do —
He expected to hear a Greek chorus.

The **gorgeous** young actress, Veronica,
Is hailed from New York to Salonika,
For her wit and her wiles,
Her great purr, and big smiles,
And her wonderfully curved "anatomica."

A **hunter** from far off Uganda,
Built a tree perch to spy on a panda;
Panda sneaked up behind,
Knocked him out of his blind,
And now owns a fancy veranda.

*M*id his circle of wives, spun Sheik Aram,
 Having sex in the nude with his harem;
  He'd bounce his bare pate
  Off the tits of each mate,
 As he swiveled about on the carom.

*S*aid the bishop of Withington Mews,
"I don't care if parishioners snooze.
But it's awfully unfair
When I lead them in prayer,
To be snoring so loud in the pews."

*T*hat rascal they call Robin Hood,
Was a little bit misunderstood;
To the King, he was bad,
To the poor, a fine lad,
But Maid Marion found him "real good."

*M*iss Morris will greatly enthuse,
O'er the benefits rare of a cruise;
She has wherewithal
To enjoy ports of call,
And hot sex with each crewman she'll choose.

$\mathcal{A}$**s the animals** boarded the Ark,
Old man Noah was heard to remark:
"You rabbits and mink
Behave or we'll sink,
No fucking allowed on this bark!"

Ancient Greeks really feared their god Zeus,
Who oft showered them with abuse;
Lightning bolts and reports
Would convey angry thoughts,
But at times meant his bowels were loose.

Said the old boy "I've long let it pass,
But the news has now proven, alas,
'Twas no anal inspection,
But a goddam erection,
That sergeant once shoved up my ass!"

A hot tempered tailor named Nick,
Made a suit undeniably slick;
When its owner said: "Botch —
It's too tight in the crotch!"
Nick cut off two-thirds of his prick.

To her neighbors, said Mrs. Hernandez,
"No guy does less work than my man does.
　　I can shout and complain,
　　But it all is in vain,
Nothing helps like a kick in his can does."

The writer said, "I'm telling you,
Our values are really askew;
      When a bench player takes
      More 'n the President makes,
We've got some rethinking to do!"

Each day now, the star girls and boys,
Use pre-nuptial agreements as ploys,
      So that in their divorce,
      Which will soon come, of course,
Each gets something back for their "joys."

Some girls promise love with their eyes;
Some girls promise love with deep sighs;
      But I can't resist
      Those girls who insist
On proving their love 'twixt their thighs.

*N*ewlyweds flying night coach in Spain,
Cuddled close in the dark of the plane,
When a sudden air pocket
Pulled piston from socket —
They'd've been far better off on the train!

***F*rom his window,** the lecherous pastor
Saw a mob that he knew spelled disaster,
For he'd buried his cock
In most wives in his flock,
He could run, but their husbands run faster!

*P*reacher shouted, "God's wrath and Hell's fire
Await those steeped in carnal desire."
  But the way he would ravish
  Sister Mary MacTavish,
Made you feel he was much of a liar!

*T*hey should make it a national rule,
That the man's an incredible fool,
  Who will risk every life —
  In sex, not with his wife —
With no condom adorning his tool.

*W*ith a dear friend, this pregnant gal, Sue,
Discussed a young preacher they knew;
  Said Sue, "You can see
  What the guy's done to me;
Now, tell me what he's done to you."

A **most talented** call girl, Doreen,
Is beloved by all men she has seen;
  Besides cunt, tit, and ass,
  Her advice was first class,
With good humor well laid in between.

T **he gang** at the fetishists' ball,
Had fun as their photos recall;
  Most wore rubber or leather,
  Some were pulled on a tether,
And some wore near nothing at all!

A **conceited** young swordsman named Roy,
Felt his cock was his pride and his joy;
  But a hooker we know,
  Who'd seen men come and go,
Told him, "That thing, my boy, is a toy!"

"**My new stunt**," said kink mistress Marium,
"Is to sit johns right in my aquarium,
　　Where each creature crawls
　　Over his cock and balls,
Some bite, and some sting, so I vary 'em."

47

On the corner each night, guys would dally,
'Round the neighborhood sexpot named Sally;
They'd need no bed or car
To make out with this "star,"
'Cause she'd do it right there in the alley!

A **handsome** young farm boy named James,
Was always a hit with the dames,
'Cause he'd certainly show
Just how he'd plow a row,
And besides that knew other fun games.

S **aid** a sugar-mapling farmer, "I see
My taps pour more sap than should be;
And with my bad luck, it's
Overflowing my buckets,
So the sap running here includes me!"

A **sexy** street walker, Yolanda,
Took this john to her cozy veranda;
But when she asked pay
For a really great lay,
He jumped up and read her "Miranda."

𝓘n their pick-up, twin farm boys conspire
On a tactic of which they don't tire;
Mike drives, while twin, Jack,
Beds a girl in the back —
Country roads push sensations much higher!

*M*ost **street-walking** gals act real nice,
They're yours in your car for a price;
So, guys who are fast,
And don't want love to last,
Can get laid and back home in a trice.

*T*his **openly** sexy young flower,
Wore sharp metal clothes by the hour,
Saying, "Points that are shiny
Scare guys who are whiny,
But win me the men with real power."

A **hopeful** young swordsman named Cecil,
Loved the feel of his cock near her vessel;
And so he was quick,
To answer real slick,
Ads by gals who were willing to wrestle!

*F*etishists Don and Louise really treasure,
Dressing up for their sexual pleasure;
They'll first debate whether
It'll be latex or leather,
With harnesses all made to measure!

Said the Duke with the delicate air,
  "For my three upstairs maids I don't care;
    But my pleasure and joy,
    Is my Spanish house-boy,
  With his invitingly plump derrière!"

Bruce claims he gets real constipated,
But with sodomy never is sated;
Too often, I fear,
There's a cock up his rear,
I'll take bets those two facts are related!

It's not easy for me to say whether
You've met Jules, who's addicted to leather,
He's so wrapped up in hide,
You can't tell who's inside,
But they lead "him" about on a tether.

The Englishman often enjoys,
His fondness for buggering boys,
Which accounts for his pallor,
But hardly his valor,
And certainly not for his poise!

"When I die," said old Angus McLeod,
"Bury me in my kilt, and no shroud;
    'Twill make the girls sad,
    Should they lift up my plaid,
At the death of a man so endowed!"

A tight anus had Alexis, the Greek,
And sodomy caused him to shriek,
    'Til his lover, so loyal,
    Found some fresh olive oil,
Now they couple with nary a squeak.

The stud who is now into cruising,
Some street-walking gal will be choosing;
    But, he's gonna be had,
    'Cause back at her pad,
Her pimp waits to give him a bruising.

$\mathcal{T}$**he guy** who rents videos-to-go,
Has great flicks lined up in each row,
But makes the most cash
From his well-hidden stash,
Of sex films, for those in the know!

To the bishop, confessed Miss McNaught,
"I've been dallying more than I ought.
      But, is it a sin
      To take strangers in,
The Bible says do so, I thought?"

Your ad called you "successful, romantic,
Most caring, and never pedantic;"
      Then how come it's true,
      When I'm out with you,
Your self-love is driving me frantic?

Said the famed model, "Any confection
Is terrible for my complexion;
      And Doc says that raw meat
      I should use as a treat,
So, hand me your stunning erection!"

$\mathcal{A}$n **amorous** fellow name Fife,
Bought tight latex drawers for his wife;
Saying, "I'll try this tack,
To tighten her crack,
And put 'snap' in our failing love life."

EXECUTIVE DECISION

*T*he **"Chairman"** was endlessly feared,
By his staff, much respected, revered;
　　But longed in his soul
　　To reverse that role,
To be mastered, his dignity speared.

*H*e **said** to himself, "If today
　To a floor sweeper's role I'd essay,
　　It'd just be a laugh
　　To my hard-working staff,
There has got to be some other way."

A **dominatrix** he then found,
Who soon had him helplessly bound,
　　And, most happily,
　　He'd obey her, as she
Had him kneeling right there on the ground.

$\mathscr{A}$**nd so** ends our brief little tale
Of this take-charge, responsible, male;
Whose Freudian soul,
Says, "At times, switch that role,
To remain psychologically hale."

There's an over-ambitious cock-sucker,
Whose mouth grew so wide it won't pucker;
Since she can't keep control
Of each gentleman's pole,
Guys rarely stop by now to fuck her.

Her accountant told rich Mrs. Spalling,
"Pay your taxes, and quit all the stalling,
Or you'll take a real bath,
If it's up to the wrath,
Of the IRS when they come calling."

A lusty young sexpot named Vicky,
With lovers was always most picky,
She'd let only the best
Spend a night in her nest,
All the rest ever got was a quickie!

The organ of "Flasher" McSlote,
Was far too immense for Deep Throat,
  And therefore instead
  Of girls who gave head,
He kept an obliging young goat.

The big blonde, doing laps, swims on by,
Lifeguard "Muscles," he catches her eye;
    Now, on his "breaks," we gather
    They screw to a lather —
Gym club romance is hard to deny!

Said the duck hunter, deep in his blind,
"I'm freezing my legs and behind;
    I've got decoys out there,
    But can see ducks nowhere,
Those bastards are reading my mind!"

A **lusty** young ad man named Milt,
Had an eye for those girls who were built;
    And in truth it was they
    Who could not keep away,
'Cause he'd fill them, but never with guilt.

The **loving** in London was prime;
The screwing in Sydney, sublime;
    But who could forget
    The raw sex and real sweat,
From three New York girls at one time!

A **fair lass** who secretly watches
The bulk and the heft of men's crotches,
Says, "I'd like to stare,
But really don't dare,
'Cause I break out in very strange splotches."

T **he fate** of the dread Berlin Wall,
Is certainly wise to recall;
Most was ground into bits,
Used to line drainage pits,
But some floors an elephant's stall.

W **ith girls,** Tom sought rapid advancement,
So he went in for penile enhancement;
Now, the size of his cock
Puts his best dates in shock —
He's still learning what "taking a chance" meant!

$\mathcal{C}$**rusaders** leaving to soon risk their lives,
Locked chastity belts on their wives,
And left salve for the itches
Caused by iron-clad britches —
Too bad if they came down with hives!

"*Fuck* Goliath," said David, "I smote him,"
But the Scriptures he then said misquote him;
"I didn't aim at his head,
As they tell you, instead,
I hit the prick with a brick in his scrotum!"

During church, the refined Bob and Pru,
Sit demure as can be in their pew;
But, when out of sight —
Which is most every night —
Oh my Gawd what the two of them do!

So incredibly sexy was Nancy,
She could make many thousand men "antsy,"
But only would spend
Time with each treasured friend,
In frolic more funny than fancy!

When the Deacon Orrin McSpeak
Baptized a young girl in the creek,
As he lowered her down,
She reached under his gown,
And gave his firm scepter a tweak.

A **sweating** young harlot named Rhoda,
Smiled up at the gent who bestrode her,
Saying, "I'll drop the price
If you send out for ice,
And order some scotch and some soda."

The faulty young tenor, McGuire,
To top notes could only aspire;
'Til his teacher, Miss Stutz,
Kicked him right in the nuts,
Now he sings not falsetto, but higher.

The transvestites today aim to please,
Offer "best of both worlds" for their fees,
They've built round tits and ass,
Looks and legs that will pass,
And hide large cocks that jump to a squeeze!

A lumberjack out in Gaspé,
Found Rose an exceptional lay;
Her movements were limber,
And she would shout "timber,"
When his pole was about to give way.

*W*hen in Minnesota, Miss Gold
Used long johns to ward off the cold;
But they had a rear door,
Which she frequently wore
Unbuttoned for friends, I am told.

To his henchmen, The Devil did tell,
"There are guys who're too lousy for Hell;
Some names I could mention,
Don't rate my attention,
So I'm building a crummy sub-cell."

A **lovely** young lass, name of Lyder,
Was wooed by a scoundrel name Schneider;
Though she swore a brief pet
Was as far as he'd get,
She wound up with Schneider inside 'er!

S **aid** the steward, "The heck with your view,
You'd know if you frequently flew;
In the past I would tell
Guys like you 'Go to hell!'
But I hear there's 'No Smoking' there, too!"

T **here was** an old harlot from Perth,
Who'd fuck you for all you were worth;
While all arts she'd employ,
There was naught to enjoy,
She was utterly lacking in mirth.

Cellar lights of the weird Mr. Drabors,
Raised suspicions about his nights' labors;
And, if folks, in fact,
Had witnessed his act,
They'd've found him dissecting two neighbors.

So busy is call girl, Liz Leeper,
To catch her you must buzz her beeper;
And, while guys would delight
In having her the whole night,
Most spring for two hours, 'cause it's cheaper.

As the crew built the lodge for Miss Grayson,
She and a carpenter, nude, were embracin';
She urged, "Turn me about,
And shoot me your grout,"
Said he, "Sorry, Ma'am, you want a mason!"

To her husband, said Mrs. O'Brien,
"Give up those sex toys you've been buyin';
For those things I don't care,
Just shove it in there,
And act not like a wimp, but a lion!"

The vagina of Abigail Tittle,
From non-use became very brittle;
When horny old Fred
Enticed her to bed,
He got in, but he cracked it a little.

An eminent author named Guy,
Tells of outfits and leaders that lie;
Citing what they would do
When in full public view,
And things they would do on the sly!

It's the story you hear around town,
From folks who in Math class would drown;
So you just have to wait,
To discover your fate,
For they'll say, "Our computer is down!"

$\mathcal{T}$**he alumni** continued to gather,
Fifty years since they raised quite a lather;
A sexy waitress walked by,
One man said with a sigh,
"I'd like that, and to miss all this blather!"

OWED TO A HEAD NURSE

A **cranky** old buzzard named Mills,
Was hospitalized for weird ills;
His stomach gave growls,
He had aches and cramped bowels,
Alternating with fevers and chills.

The doctors all tried to help Mills,
And engaged in a battle of wills,
　　　Trying all medications,
　　　Debating operations,
While prescribing great batches of pills.

Mills' condition continued to wane,
The medics were going insane,
　　　When a sexy head nurse
　　　Said they couldn't do worse
Than try her way of easing his pain.

She climbed into bed with old Mills,
Used her body to ward off his chills,
　　　And ran her smooth hands
　　　Over penis and glands,
Caressing all valleys and hills.

His recovery wasn't too quick,
But there seemed to be life in his prick,
So she thought, with some luck,
If I give it a suck,
That gambit might just turn the trick.

So she nibbled the end of his cock,
Still his tensions refused to unlock,
Then she started to hum,
Which might cause him to come,
As back and forth gently she'd rock.

First she tried pretty "Molly Malone,"
In a gentle and languorous tone,
But, as much as she'd go
With "Alive, alive, oh!,"
Mills would simply just lie there and moan.

*N*ext she ventured an aria from "Carmen,"
With results that were truly alarmin',
     The pace of the song,
     Gave life to his dong,
Nurse checked to make sure she's not harmin!

*T*he aches and the pains of old Mills,
Went swiftly away with his chills,
As she mastered her trick
And all 'round his prick,
Her tongue would beat time with her trills.

*S*o much for the medicos wise,
Their notions, and potions, and whys;
While their great erudition
Helps most folks' condition,
At times they just can't get a rise.

*A*nd to help these last patients pull through it,
Takes the skill of the nurses who do it;
So the peak of my praise
Goes to them on those days
When they eagerly put their heads to it!

"You're terrific!"

To a driller, this comely young belle
Said, "Searching for water is hell.
    Come to my little plot,
    Sink the pipe that you've got,
And we'll pump 'til you bring in the well."

A most handsome ad man called "Muns,"
Was outspoken, quick, and no dunce;
    But the loving he'd get,
    From the girls that he met,
He never would mention, not once!

A husky young plumber named Larry,
Was asked by a fair lass to tarry;
    He said, "Sure I will,
    And I'll give you a thrill,
Just don't ever ask me to marry!"

$\mathcal{H}$**is true love** said, "I'm in the mood,
Just cover my hot spots with food;
    You can lick every bit
    Of whipped cream off my tit,
And tongue pears up me, too, if you're shrewd."

A **charming** young devil was Franky,
Loved dancing, was fun, never cranky;
But, it wasn't his twirls
That endeared him to girls,
'Twas his passion for real hanky-panky!

*N***o wonder** the porky sex clubber,
Stays away from tight suits made of rubber;
For while it's fact that
They'll stretch over the fat,
They sure as hell won't hide that blubber!

*T***here once was** a stud named LoMeter,
Who lost all the strength in his peter;
But, he knew without fail,
As he looked at each quail,
He still had the passion to eat 'er!

*N*ow, **Mochlos,** a horny old Greek,
Would hunt in each sex toy boutique,
For a novel extender
To his well-worn male gender,
That'd make all the whorehouse girls shriek!

$\mathcal{A}$ **farm girl** by name of McSprattle,
Was addicted to sucking-off cattle,
'Til a bull from the South
Shot a load in her mouth,
That made both her ovaries rattle!

They knew him as weird "Mr. X,"
Whose thing was some really wild sex;
But the girls didn't mind
The kink outfits he'd find,
'Cause he paid them in cash, never checks.

The goatherd, a lad name of Motta,
Confessed to his sister, Carlotta,
"Fucking goats that are lame,
Will for sure bring us shame,
But still, if you gotta, you gotta!"

There was a young man from South Bend,
Whose cock had a sandpaper end;
Each gal he took fishin',
Soon wound up by wishin'
Her vagina would readily mend.

The **bulk** of Corinthia Quayle,
Went four-sixty-two on the scale;
 But the sailor who found her,
 Said he's happy to pound her,
"It's just like harpooning a whale!"

Aunt Alice has such immense thighs,
That no matter which way she lies,
    Men would need an extender
    At the end of their gender,
To get at her copious prize.

(however...)

Her lover was Harry McTeas,
Whose cock hangs right down past his knees;
    And he won't ever say
    How he stretched it that way,
But for Alice, he's sure built to please.

A quick man with his cock is ol' Blotzer,
And no lass can escape 'fore he pots her;
    But what's earned him acclaim,
    And spread world-wide his fame,
Is the ten yards head start that he spots her.

The **back room** of Dom's delicatessen
Is used by the staff for undressin',
 They play games in the nude
 While they make the day's food,
What's in their paté I'm not guessin'!

A **creative** director named Hy,
Is a truly incredible guy;
    Men struggle to gain
    The things in his brain,
The women, the thing in his fly!

A **fussy** cock-sucker named Grace,
Called Angelo's balls a disgrace,
    "They've got varicose veins,
    And some black and brown stains,
And what's more, they hang in my face!"

A **couple** we know, much maligned,
Call "phone sex" when they're so inclined;
    With a speaker they own
    They expand each kink tone,
And act out what's then brought to mind.

The lovers of horny Aunt Maude,
Find their backs indescribably clawed
From her frenzy, as they
Fucked the usual way —
If they tried "soixante-neuf," oh my Gawd!

A **promiscuous** friend of Aunt Mame,
Was a more than peculiar dame,
With a digital watch
Up the slit in her crotch,
Which would show the true time that you came.

S **aid Sue,** "I'm in need of some pills,
To cure my mysterious ills;
For every time, Doc,
I am shown a hot cock,
I somehow come down with the chills!"

T **he young** Army nurse at Fort Ord,
Found spirits were low in her ward.
Now she spends just a while
In each bed 'long the aisle,
And morale has predictably soared!

A **maid** from an area tropic,
Was more than severely myopic;
    She thought Easter egg hues
    Were bath salts she could use,
And emerged from her tub kaleidoscopic.

Said the wise actress to her new date,
"If much later tonight we do mate,
I've had more than enough
Of the kinky sex stuff,
And look forward to doing it straight!"

Those **who** use drugs as "pure recreation,"
Pose a disabling threat to our nation,
Since their growing addiction
Spells helpless affliction,
When we need smarts for our preservation.

All **stock brokers** hate clients who
Call frequently to get their view,
Of issues they say
They will give a big play,
Then somehow just don't follow through!

$\mathcal{S}$**aid** a stock broker's girl friend named Toots,
"You're a wise guy who just pussy-foots;
    I'm tired of your 'calls,'
    You've got cock and balls,
Now, get with it, and give me some 'puts'."

*T*he **new** rural mailman named Cox,
From a farm girl received two quick shocks;
"Out here," said this quail,
"You'll deliver the 'male,'
And stuff it right into my box!"

A **canny** old whore from Fredonia,
Pulled an act that just couldn't be phoney-a;
　　Guys thought her pantin' and wheezin'
　　Meant their cocks were so pleasin',
In truth, she had triple pneumonia!

Farmer **Seth** is one hell of a dowser,
With that long thing that hangs in his trouser;
　　It won't seek ground water,
　　As some say it ought-ter,
But it'll sure spot a virgin and rouse her!

The **verse** about farmer McGork,
Who loved to let pigs suck his dork,
　　I can't quite remember,
　　But since last September
I've lost my desire for pork.

*S*aid a mischievous madam named Carmen,
"I really don't see any harm in
　　　　Kissin' an' huggin'
　　　　An' pettin' and fuggin',
But my neighbors all find it alarmin'."

*B*eloved by all madams was Ace,
Who demanded two girls in each place;
　　　　His sport called for one
　　　　To suck 'til he'd done,
While the other one sat on his face.

*S*aid the police chief, "This Asian massage,
Is really a rather old dodge,
　　　　For a prostitutes' ring
　　　　That's been doing its thing,
And we're trying like hell to dislodge."

A **prosperous** madam named Lou,
Explained to her diligent crew,
"You just can't make out right
Seeing ten johns a night,
Spend time with the real well-to-do."

*T*he **prissy** old spinster, Miss Hodger,
Fears most she'll be raped by her lodger;
    And so each night she lies,
    A steel trap 'twixt her thighs,
Which she's certain will catch the old codger.

*S*aid Roxy, the savvy masseuse,
"My massage parlor bit is a ruse;
    Those suckers will pay
    In hopes of a lay,
But from me all they get is a goose."

*T*he **cunt** of a whore name of Sprockett,
Has many a velvet lined pocket,
    Each one shaped to the size
    Of her regular guys,
If *you* haven't tried it, don't knock it!

*T*he **bar scene** at Alain's Karaoke,
Is cluttered, and noisy, and smoky;
　　But, some folks who can sing,
　　Give real style to their thing,
While others turn out to be croaky.

A **lecherous** golfer named Huff,
Wouldn't quit when his lass cried "Enough!;"
He tried going one-up
So she shifted her cup,
His next stroke was played in the rough.

*A***s her husband,** so sleepy, withdrew,
She said, "You've become a poor screw.
The advice that you get
As you surf Internet,
I'd been hoping had rubbed off on you!"

*L***et's hear it** for sweet little Joan,
Who to sexual contact is prone;
And, if her spouse finds a way
To be with her all day,
He might keep her off of the phone!

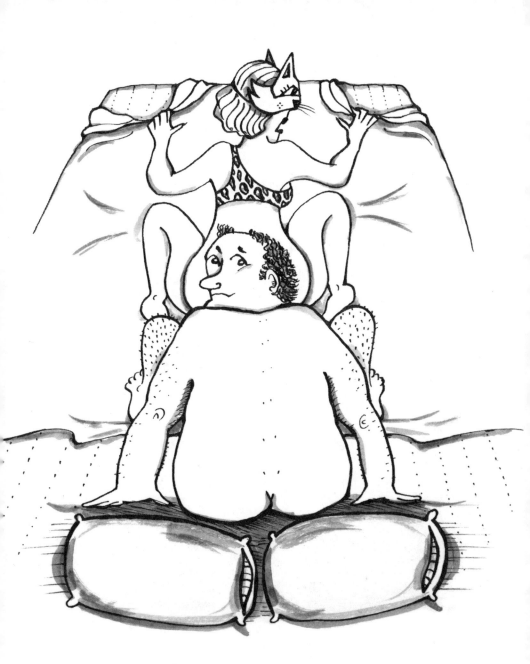

A **barrel** of fun is Rosemary,
Whose sex life is quite legendary;
And so husband, Ted,
When he takes her to bed,
Will go for positions that vary!

The fisherman chartered this yacht,
The captain was sure of his spot,
But while they did play
For sailfish all day,
Two small sharks were all that they got.

A well-known researcher named Stu,
Would watch all his other pals screw,
And then say to his mate,
"They are so out of date,
Forget them, let's try something new."

A horny young salesman named Otto,
Won a $35 mil jackpot Lotto;
So he bought a big yacht,
Took all hookers he'd spot,
And sailed off to a hedonist grotto.

Harry's girls

Harry's yacht is equipped with twin screws,
An expression that boat owners use;
Except in this case
It's twins Beth and Grace,
Whom he's having aboard for the cruise.

$\mathcal{S}$**ome clients** just love to play games,
With creditors, employees, and dames;
And use my legal talents
To help keep their balance,
And court records free of their names!

Said the lawyer, "Professionally,
I find irksome, especially,
   Those clients who're prone
   To keep me on the phone,
As they strive to get answers for free."

The lawyers will always get chills,
From clients who don't pay their bills,
But feel they've the right
To call up day or night,
And talk endlessly 'bout all their ills.

Your "Role Play" ad promises much,
"A sensuous, sensitive, touch;"
But most guys who'll incline
To put dough on the line,
Are hoping for blow jobs, as such.

Dear Edward says he'd like to clone
Certain show girls whose work he has known,
So that on any night
He was feeling uptight,
He could find one who'd like to be prone.

The guys who so eagerly sit,
At the ramp in the Bottomless Pit,
    Stare at strippers who dance,
    Minus bra, minus pants,
And show acres of cunt and loose tit.

The screwball who dared water-ski,
At midnight, when no one could see,
Caught a protruding rock
Right smack in his jock,
Now he has to sit down to make pee.

"Someone help me!" wailed poor Mr. Plum,
"Wife's fetish is driving me numb.
It's them beads of brass
She shoves up my ass,
And yanks one by one 'til I come!"

Said husband to wife, "Do have reason,
This thermometer game just ain't pleasin';
You lower the spot,
'Cause you say you're too hot,
And then I push it up 'cause I'm freezin!"

*T*he **great sex** on late night TV,
Is just so entrancing to see,
But I then find that I'm
Always fresh outta time,
To get you to do that to me!

*A*n **Apache** who fought for Cochise,
Kept two of his teepees for lease;
He'd rent by the hour
Each squaw-equipped bower,
And for orgies supplied his young niece.

118

*T*he fantastically well-built Miss Platt,
Would make love at the drop of a hat;
    She had nerve, she had verve,
    And was eager to serve,
You can't ask for better than that.

*S*aid a wond'rous old being on Mars,
As he viewed Earth's new flights to the stars,
    "Those folks really show
    They've a long way to go,
'Cause their robots look like antique cars."

*T*he scientist suffered dejection
From his lover's final rejection;
    He was told to "Get lost!,"
    Built a bomb at great cost
And flew off in every direction!

The patients of dear Doctor "D,"
Said a prime periodontist was he,
And so did each maid
That he happily laid,
'Cause he checked their whole bodies for free!

The guy who says "No anesthetic,"
To dentists ain't macho-athletic,
Just one who is scared,
When a needle is bared,
Which today, they regard as pathetic.

The patient for whom I least care,
As soon as he sits in my chair,
Announces that he
Must go somewhere to pee,
While the waiting room waits in despair."

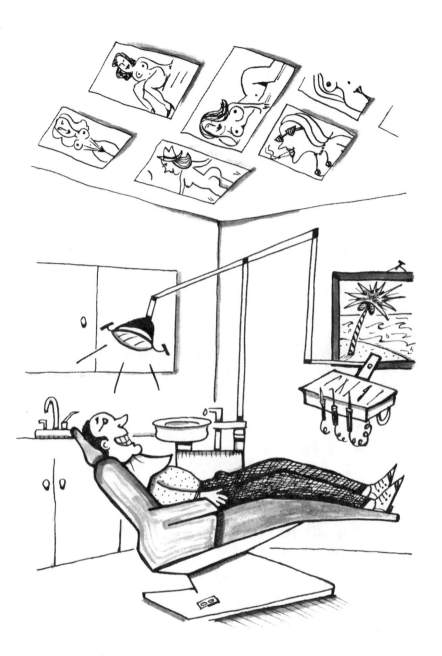

*N*ow, Debbie's a lady with feeling,
Hygienist whose manner's appealing;
Male patients she'll see,
Will be shown to Room 3,
Where nude centerfolds cover the ceiling!

The guy who was sometimes called Chicker,
　　Would ply girls with very fine liquor,
　　　　So, with no inhibitions,
　　　　They would try all positions,
　　And then do it straight as a kicker.

The exec's great assistant, named Cher,
　　Could be trusted, was quick, ever fair;
　　　　But the things that she'd do,
　　　　When her work day was through,
　　With her partner would sure curl your hair!

The build of Miss Mount is incredible,
　　Her legs she makes instantly spreadable;
　　　　And, between you and me,
　　　　And her nether goatee,
　　Her pussy's deliciously edible!

$\mathcal{H}$**ere's to** the world of fine whiskey,
For those who don't find it too risky;
It lightens your cares,
It sparks love affairs,
And otherwise helps you feel frisky.

A **big man** with his bat is Pete Jagger,
For his ball club he's never a lagger;
And for fun he will orgy
With Beth, Sue and Georgie,
On the team, he is known as "Three-bagger!"

*A*t bat, he was never a "whiffer,"
Got hits, so his team named him "Biffer;"
Which pleases his wife,
Who, in their married life,
Calls him that when she wants him much stiffer.

A true baseball fan know as Ira,
Has got one most secret admire-a,
She'll watch his young frame
As he follows each game,
In the hope that he'll see and desire-a."

*T*o the baseball star, said his young wife,
"Enough of your glamorous life,
You best come home, instead
Of being with girls you bed,
Or I'll cut that thing off with a knife!"

Fumed the astronaut, who lectured a bit,
"My audiences don't vary one whit;
    You would think they'd be keen
    On what we've done, mapped, and seen,
But they first want to know how we shit!"

The abnormally shy Mr. Jett,
Loves chat rooms on the Internet;
    When asked if he'd made
    Any dates to get laid?
He answered most boldly, "You bet!"

A drunk electrician named Walls,
Couldn't stand the heat from his balls;
    Hooked a transistorized fan
    'Neath his shorts, but oh man,
It cuts his nuts each time he falls.

A **computer** salesman named Clive,
Says: "On the horniest women, I thrive;
    For, they can't resist,
    And, even insist,
When I tell 'em it comes with 'hard drive'!"

*Y*ears after she got her divorce,
Golfer's ex-wife did suffer remorse;
  She lured him to bed,
  Spread her legs wide, and said:
"Thought you might like to play the Old Course!"

'*N*eath the pile-up, the world famous "rugger,"
Said with menace to the nearest tugger,
  "Get your guys off of me,
  Or else when I count three,
There's a bloke here I'm going to bugger!"

A lady third baseman named Hunt,
Perfected a marvelous stunt,
  She would take a deep crouch,
  And, with nary an "ouch,"
She would field ground balls with her...
       bare hands.

*S*aid the pro golfer on the 8th tee,
   "Omigod, how I do have to pee!
      Now what can I do,
      The TV camera's in view,
   And I'm dribbling down past my knee!"

*T*he **Amazon** tribe worshipped Reymos,
A Brooklyn born stud they made famous;
"'Cause the average dong
With us dykes won't last long —
Takes a big guy like Reymos to tame us."

A **sexy** young artist named Judi,
Said work often left her so moody,
That she'd quit for a day,
Just to find guys who'd play,
'Cause her spirits revived with a "nudie."

A **promiscuous** plumber named Chuck,
Tried tapping a virgin for luck;
But their rapid communion
Heat-bonded their union,
And his overworked joiner got stuck.

The **suave** guy with girl friend in tow,
Went to swap clubs he thought he did know,
And admitted to fun,
Doing things he had done,
But was pissed that she left all aglow!

$\mathcal{P}$**at's supermart** was empty that day,
And the produce lad eager to play,
   So, with her derrière
   Perched on grape, peach and pear,
They made fruit cup their own special way!

A **curious** stud, name of Irving,
    Most call girls would find quite unnerving,
        'Cause when each had his pole
        Well in reach of their goal,
    He'd choose to do something self-serving!

*T*he **ad said** "Swell guy, with pizzazz,"
    After dating, she gave him the razz,
        For she found, instead,
        What "swelled" was his head,
    And pizzas are all that he has!

A **coast-to-coast** business has Patchin,
    Which requires a great deal of "batchin';"
        And we think that he
        Found a promiscuous "she,"
    'Cause we've noticed he does lots of scratchin'!

*T*he **great** charm of France he now preaches,
He lectures, sometimes even teaches,
But won't want you to know
His real reason to go,
Is to see lovely nudes on its beaches.

*I*n **the love** life of Ruthie and Robby,
Finding new spots to screw is their hobby;
You can imagine the look
That the staid doorman took,
At such goings-on right in his lobby!

A coked-up young driver named Phil,
Tried to pass going up a blind hill;
O'er the top came a car,
And the crash was bizarre,
They've found most of his car, not of Phil.

In the mind of Abigail Hite,
Rape causes incredible fright,
So she shoves a cow bell
'Twixt the lips of her well,
Which clanks when she turns in the night.

The great gift of muff-diver Nilde,
Is a tongue that just drives the girls wild;
And, they all agree,
"It's great fun for me,
And there's no fear of having a child!"

The psychiatrist known as "Doc" Mason,
At work is reserved, self-effacin';
But that's just his style,
Which is wrong by a mile,
You should see when his wife he's embracin'!

The outspoken Earl of Gallay,
Was heard by his valet to say,
"Costume balls are a bore,
But I'll go just once more,
And with luck I'll find someone to lay."

"Doc" Harvey's a debonair guy,
Suave, handsome, a glint in his eye!
So, it's not just his care
For their infants' welfare
That's made many a young mother sigh!

$\mathcal{A}$ **fine dentist** is good Doctor Browne,
Who labored in making a crown,
    Which, when it was tested,
    His patient ingested,
Now they'll wait for its exit "downtown."

Offices where proctologists practice,
As a rule, will not likely attract us;
And, if young Dr. Cone
Feels especially alone,
Check his reception room, potted with cactus!

All dentists do hate the big bragger,
Who comes in with much of a swagger,
And mocks the affair,
'Til he's set in the chair,
And turns out to be their worst "gagger."

Doc sits in his office aswarm,
With paperwork he must conform,
And, due to this, he
Doesn't give you or me,
Time for good he was trained to perform.

$\mathcal{A}$ **computer** expert named Stout,
Received a furious clout,
  From the cop on the beat,
  As he strolled down the street,
For it seemed that his input hung out!

The champion weight-lifter, Rawls,
Has a rare act that always enthralls,
He will take a deep crouch,
Get a grip on his pouch,
And hoist himself up by his balls.

Her hand on his cock was a clue,
Her tongue in his ear made it two,
And her puckered-up mouth
Made it clear, north or south,
There'd be fun in whatever they do.

A pretty young call girl, Yvette,
Was great friends with each man she met,
'Cause she'd slip and she'd slide,
And still hold you inside,
And do you as good as you'll get.

A **lusty** young stud name of Dodd,
Thought screwing in hammocks was mod,
And so did wife, Mickey,
Who'd join for a quickie,
But the neighbors all thought it quite odd!

*S*aid hot Hazel to horny ol' Chuck,
"It's not fair that you ask me to suck.
    For I find if I do,
    When it comes time to screw,
You leave me just plumb out of luck."

*E*mphysema has spoiled poor Miss Trucks,
As a call girl she'd earned the big bucks;
    Because of her cough,
    Her business dropped off,
Now she wheezes each time that she sucks.

*T*he rich widow demanded some action,
Her broker guaranteed satisfaction;
    So, she had her way,
    And their roll in the hay,
Left the poor bastard lying in traction!

*T*he **wild** serve of "Slammer" McSput,
Hit his partner smack in her butt,
   So she signaled for time,
   Marched to colleague in crime,
And quick-kicked him in his left nut.

*N*ow here's to the life that's exciting,
And here's to each lass, so inviting,
And, here's to the cup
That's full when we sup,
And the best of friends reuniting.

Appendix

In my Introduction I promised to reproduce on these pages the dozen limericks (authors anonymous) that were sung in "The Little Nass" at Key and Seal Club on Princeton party weekends. These were sung by individual members (and were known to many) with the whole group present joining in on the chorus between each limerick verse, using a tune resembling "Cielito Lindo," which went

> "Iy, yi, yi-yi! —
> In China they never serve chili,
>> Now, here comes another verse
>> That's worse than the other verse,
> So waltz me around again, Willie!"

Though I'm quoting twelve limericks here — as best I can remember them — they aren't reproduced in any special order or ranking, but I feel confident each was sung at least once every weekend, amid a host of others club members would offer. As I've said, the songfest — of limericks and other songs — would go on 'til the early morning hours, aided and abetted by high spirits all round.

Okay, here are the top twelve, each now at least 50 years old, and most much older than that:

> There was a young lady from Norway,
> Who hung by her heels in the doorway;
>> She shouted with glee,
>> "Oh, come look at me,
> I think I've discovered one more way!"

> There once was a couple named Kelly,
> Who were doomed to sleep belly to belly,
>> Because, in their haste,
>> They used library paste,
> Instead of petroleum jelly!

A painter named Titian McSpadder,
Posed his model on top of a ladder,
 Her position to Titian
 Suggested coition,
So he climbed up the ladder and had 'er!

A lesbian out of Khartoum
Once took a young fruit to her room,
 But first she said, "Wait —
 Now let's get this straight —
Who does what, with which, and to whom?"

There was a young nun from Peru,
Who said, when the deacon withdrew,
 "The vicar was quicker,
 And thicker, and slicker,
And four inches longer than you!"

The was an old monk from Siberia,
Whose morals were very inferior,
 He did to a nun,
 What he shouldn't have done,
And now she's a Mother Superior.

There was a young maid from Alsace,
Who had the most beautiful ass,
 It wasn't round and pink,
 As you probably think,
It was brown, had long ears, and ate grass!

There was a young man named McNair,
Who was screwing his girl on the stair,
 On the thirty-first stroke,
 The banister broke,
And he finished her off in mid-air!

There was an old whore from Detroit,
Who at screwing was very adroit,
  She could contract her vagina
  To a pinpoint, or finer,
Or stretch it as wide as a quoit!

There was a young lady named Alice,
Who used TNT for a phallus;
  They found her vagina
  In North Carolina,
And bits of her tits over Dallas.

There was an old whore named Hester,
Who said to the boys who undressed her,
  "Please, if you don't mind,
  Come in from behind,
'Cause the front is beginning to fester."

There once was a young man from Kent,
Whose cock was so long that it bent,
  So to save himself trouble,
  He put it in double,
And, instead of coming, he went.

There were oh so many more — including "The young lady from Exeter;" "The young man from Cape Horn;" "The old man from Nantucket;" "The young lady from Sparta;" "The young plumber from Leigh;" "The young man from Leeds;" etc. — but the above 12 seemed most frequently sung.

Now, in citing these well established verses, I'm making no attempt to equate this book with the wonderful compendiums listed in my Bibliography. William S. Baring-Gould and Gershon Legman, in particular, have done a magnificent job in studying the history of the limerick as a verse form. With the assistance of The New York Public Library, The Library of Congress, and the Beinecke Rare Book and Manuscript Library at Yale, along with many other sources, they have traced it possibly from ancient Greece, through Shakespeare, the return of The Irish Brigade to Limerick from France, through Edward Lear — born in 1812, and regarded as the Father and Poet Laureate of the Limerick — to the limericists of the 20th century to about 1980.

Whereas they have studied and reported on the limerick down through the ages — with many examples given — this book was conceived and written to add some 240 previously unpublished limericks, which I've created over a lifetime, to the field, a quarter of them specifically illustrated. In many I have dealt with more modern mores and current happenings, with the fond hope that some of my work will be judged worthy of retention by lovers of limericks, and will spur other writers to still further efforts over the coming years.

One point I should make — not previously referred to by compilers of limerick anthologies — is that limericks, to be successful, particularly when sung, depend heavily on easily assimilated rhyme to retain their unique character. An anonymous poet has written of the limerick's nature and strict format —

> The limerick packs laughs anatomical,
> Into space that is quite economical,
>> But the good ones I've seen,
>> So seldom are clean,
> And the clean ones so seldom are comical.

In truth, then, to have some meaningful text rhyme within the daunting confines of the limerick form, requires the use of a sizable and current vocabulary.

Back in 1775 when Sam Johnson compiled the first great modern "Dictionary of the English Language," it contained only about 50,000 terms. Fifty years later, Noah Webster's "American Dictionary of the English Language " saw an increase of 50% to 75,000 terms. But, today's average college dictionary contains some 180,000 entries, with 250,000 definitions. Which means that — with increased education, technology, women's activities, world travel, space exploration, etc. — our language has become correspondingly enlarged. And with it more and new opportunity for rhyme relating to all the foregoing, and the sexual activities and current mores energized by them.

I look forward to other limericists making the most of this continued growth.

Bibliography

When you've had a fascination for limericks as long as I have — reading and writing them since the late 1930s — it's really impossible to provide a full bibliography at this point, bringing into focus where I saw what. I feel certain that in the early days I saw limericks in *The Saturday Evening Post,* and *Liberty,* magazines I delivered door to door. Later, I probably spied some in *The Wall Street Journal,* in early issues of *Playboy,* and in compendiums of poetry, by many authors, old and new, I've read over the years, including those of Ogden Nash, Berton Braley, Morris Bishop, Isaac Asimov and John Ciardi.

Certainly many — authors unknown — were sung at Key and Seal Club at Princeton, as previously noted. And, I've seen limericks assembled in regionally issued volumes, also in countries as far away as Australia, and submitted during contests. Unfortunately, I never kept an ongoing file, which would be of possible interest to the true limerick lover — the good ones remain lodged in my brain.

However, there have been books published exclusively devoted to limericks that I've gone through over the years, and some I have kept in my library. For insight into the development of the limerick form of verse, some extensive bibliographies, and some excellent examples, I commend to the limerick lover these volumes:

The Lure of the Limerick, by William S. Baring-Gould; Clarkson N. Potter, Inc. publisher; distributed by Crown Publishers, Inc. First published in 1967, at least 14 printings. Published again in 1989, in larger size, by Wordsworth Editions Ltd., Ware, Hertfordshire, England. A compilation of over 500 poems.

The Limerick, edited by Gershon Legman. Copyright 1964 and 1969. 1700 examples, published by Bell Publishing Company, a division of Crown Publishers, Inc. A compilation.

More Limericks, edited by Gershon Legman. Copyright 1977. 2750 more examples. Published by Bell in 1980. A compilation.

Out on a Limerick, edited and copyright 1960 by Bennett Cerf. Over 300 limericks compiled. Published by Harper & Row.

Limericks: Too Gross — 291 original off-color limericks by Isaac Asimov and John Ciardi. Copyright 1978. Published by W. W. Norton & Company, Inc.

The Richard Erdoes Illustrated Treasury of Classic Unlaundered Limericks. Introduction by Isaac Asimov. Some 220 limericks compiled. Copyright 1984. Balsam Press.

3024 Dirty Limericks — Original limericks by Albin Chaplin. Copyright 1983. Publisher: Bell.

The limerick aficionado who wants to trace their history, and read thousands of limericks, should turn to these long existing sources, particularly the first two mentioned. The late Clement Wood — American poet, author, critic and poetry teacher — has stated that "The limerick is the only fixed form (of verse) indigenous to the English language." What I have attempted to do here is to add 240+ new, original, quality, limericks to a noteworthy class. Sure hope I've succeeded.

𝒜 **curvaceous** star model from Wales,
Loved to lie beneath husky young males,
"In that way," said she,
I can put weight on me,
And not have it show on the scales."

Acknowledgments

This book, and the limericks it includes, has been assembled from original work I've done over most of my life, so I'm sure to forget some good soul who has spurred me on to see these "ditties" brought to light. So I'll keep the first groups listed here as units, and try to enclose everybody. Heartfelt thanks then to

My family, who, whether they agreed with a particular limerick or not, knew of my interest in them, and urged me to produce this volume. And to my wife, Barb, particularly, for putting these limericks in manageable form so I could get to the printer.

Guys and gals I've known and worked with over the years, from "CB", who typed so many of these for me many years ago, to those more recent who wanted to see this book become a reality.

Personal friends in abundance who've honored me by laughing at my verses, and sincerely cheered me on.

Valued clients of my Limerick Lane Poetryworks business, who — while working with me to develop more extensive light verse for their needs — would swap limericks with me, and await publication of this original collection.

Harry Franke, outstanding Wisconsin attorney and client, who has always enlivened our correspondence with verse of his own.

Dale Messick, world renowned creator/writer/illustrator of the widely circulated "Brenda Starr" comic strip, who called after reading about me in *The Wall Street Journal*. An ardent lover of limericks all her life, she proves — as the facing page will show — that at age 91 she still wields a powerful pen, illustrating one of my limericks that had gained her attention.

Dick Burns, my most able, affable, family lawyer, who has helped me found and work out this venture, as he has with others.

Bill Ryder, Judy Penny, and Jason Tygielski of Ryder & Schild advertising agency, who have been most helpful with ideas and execution for cover design, interior type, and advertising for this volume.

Godson/author Chris Bohjalian; editor/publisher Sheldon Meyer; authors' representative Perry Knowlton; lawyer "Tick" Semmes; art director Norbert Haber; and accountant Elliott Resnick — all for their advice, insights, and support as I prepared this fun book.

Finally, and importantly, Paula Brinkman Hughes, my most versatile illustrator, whose imagination, research, artistic talent, and unfailing good humor made a visual reality of so many of the limerick verses I have composed.

I thank you all.

Al Kracht

ORDER FORM

(For your convenience, and reproduction via copier)

Please check here _____ if you would like us to contact you with regard to possibly including *your* original, previously unpublished, humorous poem, vignette, joke, cartoon, etc., in a forthcoming book. (No book purchase, as indicated below, is required.)

Limerick Lane Press, Inc.
5 Birch Lane
Chappaqua, NY 10514
Phone: (914) 238-8720

Please send me _____ copies of "Limericks New & Naughty!" (@ $19 U.S.; $26 Canadian). Thank you.

Name: _____

Address: _____

City:_____ State: _____ Zip: _____

Telephone: (   ) _____

Sales tax:
Please add 6.75% for books shipped to a New York State address.

Shipping and Handling:
$6.00 for the first book and $2.00 for each additional book.

Payment:
Check attached _____

Credit card: AMEX _____ Visa _____ MasterCard _____

Card number: _____

Name on card: _____

Expiration date: _____ / _____